Stewardship in African-American Churches

A New Paradigm

Melvin Amerson

DISCIPLESHIP RESOURCES

P.O. BOX 340003 • NASHVILLE, TN 37203-0003
www.discipleshipresources.org

Cover design by Anessa Magras.
Interior design by PerfecType, Nashville, TN.

ISBN 088177-452-9

Library of Congress Control Number 2004112421

ACKNOWLEDGEMENTS

Anytime a person undertakes a new venture, there are always persons who assisted in someway to make it all possible. This book was my new venture, and I had a number of persons who gave to me in a variety of forms. Throughout the entire process, I was blessed by God's hand. Some prayed for me, others gave words of encouragement, and there were others who said, "God called you to write this book."

I would like to acknowledge:

My wife Michele, whom I affectionately call "Wife," who allowed me time, space, and provided much needed words of encouragement;

My parents Tommy and Loretta Amerson, who called regularly to receive progress reports on the book writing process;

Texas Methodist Foundation for the opportunity to be in ministry and serve congregations throughout the state of Texas;

Charlyne Moaning, my first finance committee chairperson at St. Lo United Methodist Church, in Houston, Texas (now Norris Chapel UMC), who gave me words of encouragement and comfort when I introduced annual stewardship pledge campaigns and other stewardship ideas to the congregation. This congregation helped me understand the definition of generosity;

My editor, George Donigian, who gave me deadlines, followed with great words of inspiration.

TABLE OF CONTENTS

FOREWORD

"The earth is the Lords and everything in it, the world, and all who live in it" (Psalm 24:1). This passage of scripture has been a verse many believers have tucked away intentionally or unconscientiously. It requires us to acknowledge God as being owner of everything and defines us simply as overseers. In God's grace we can effectively and honorably manage these resources. When the Church embraces the responsibility of living as faithful managers of God's vast resources, the community of faith will prosper.

In *Stewardship in African-American Churches: A New Paradigm*, Melvin Amerson provides theological and practical application on how the Church can develop systematic approaches to stewardship. Melvin Amerson is a strategic thinker who has become familiar with the heart of God and how to unveil the vision of stewardship. He has clearly used scripture and his experience as a pastor to seek a better understanding of Psalm 24:1 for each of us.

Melvin has led many congregations in the past decade to seeing stewardship as a heart matter. He has a delightful approach to this topic and brings it all together in a passionate manner. *Stewardship in African-American Churches: A New Paradigm* is a resource that will address questions that both laity and clergy find difficult to sometimes ask and answer.

Grace and God's precious gift of Jesus is reason enough for the African-American Church to consider how we look at stewardship.

James P. Amerson
Sr. Pastor at Simpson United Methodist Church
Austin, Texas

Chapter One

HISTORY
AND TRADITIONS

*"But the aim of such instruction is love that
comes from a pure heart, a good conscience,
and sincere faith."*

I TIMOTHY 1:5

The African-American church has a strong history
and tradition of faithful Christian stewardship. Its
history and early traditions offer incredible examples of
faith in the midst of difficult and harsh situations. Many
of the early congregations largely consisted of persons of
limited resources, but these people were generous with
what they had. In the early days of the African-American

church, prior to the great migration to northern industrial cities, the majority of members derived much of their livelihood from farming, sharecropping, and domestic labor. With limited employment options, money tended to flow slowly into the African-American community.

Since money was usually tight, support for the ministry of the local church took an appearance different from caucasian churches. Giving often centered on seasonal harvest. Often the minister was paid with food instead of money. Economic challenges made tithing or regular giving a struggle for most families. However, many members made up for their limited gifts with the giving of their time and talents.

Churches needing additions to their buildings or needing repairs often did the work themselves. The men of the church volunteered their time and talents, laying the foundations, erecting the walls, putting up roofs, installing plumbing, and painting. Women of the church prepared food and refreshments as the men labored. Sharing of skills and talent was a means of contributing and was understood as an offering to God in gratitude for the skill and talent God had bestowed upon them. Members of the congregation put their efforts together for the good of the entire church.

Many families were of limited or marginal means, so the church resorted to an assortment of programs to raise money. These programs were more than ways of raising money for the church; they provided great fellowship and drew the community together. Area churches helped sister churches with their programs. Dr. J. Lavon Kincaid, in his book *God's Faithfulness: Stewardship in the Ethnic Minority Church*, gives an account of fundraising programs in the African-American church.

> Funds in the minority local church are raised in various ways. These ways include tithing, pledging, rallies, or annual observances such as anniversaries, harvest festivals, calendar teas, birthday club teas, 50-state rallies, wedding of roses, pageants, and a smorgasbord of other activities—including bake sales, chicken dinners, fish dinners, chittling dinners, car washes, baby contests, musicals, box suppers, womanless weddings, talent and fashion shows to mention only a few. In some churches the rally has been the traditional way of raising funds. [1]

Throughout the year, rallies took place. If a church was in debt, a series of rallies and dinner sales were held to help retire the debt as quickly as possible. Rallies always had a goal of raising money, but they were also a source of competition and pride among families to raise the most money. Various groups or families came together to raise money for their church. Typically, there was some form of recognition for the group or family who raised the most money for the rally.

Recognition for contributions for special projects or programs or winning a rally was cause to be recognized by the congregation. Depending on the rally or fundraiser, titles were bestowed upon the winner, such as king, queen, prince, or princess. Further, the winner was also rewarded with an engraved plaque, or an engraved plate listed on a large plaque in the fellowship hall. Plaques with engraved plates in some churches covered the halls of the church. Giving recognition to those persons or families who raised the largest sum of money provided a source of pride and motivation, while also contributing to the ministry of the church.

Multiple offerings during a service were often the norm. First came the *Regular Offering*, which supported the operating budget. The *Penny Offering* usually supported benevolence. Small churches that met once or twice a month for worship sometimes had a *Salary Offering* to pay the pastor's salary.

In later years, when churches developed more formal budgets, some churches adopted a plan to meet the budget, which many called *dues*. The dues system works simply: Once the budget is set, the number of paying members or households in the congregation divides the amount of the budget. That amount becomes dues for the church's members. There were members who were tithers, or churches that taught and stressed tithing, but there were many who practiced and embraced a dues system of supporting the ministry of the church.[2] Even today, churches still formally and informally uphold this method of supporting the work of the church.

Over the years, many of these practices and traditions have been abandoned. The rallies and contest have dwindled. I attribute a number of changes to the fact that many church members no longer derive their livelihood from farming and domestic employment. Member employement covers the gamut, from laborers to professionals, representing the entire scope of socio-economic groups. Today, our churches increasingly teach and preach tithing and proportionate giving, and members have the financial wherewithal to support the church and the willingness to accept the biblical truths of giving.

The African-American church is still the pillar of the community. Historically, it has been one of the few independently owned and operated institutions that allowed African-Americans to claim their independence and self-sufficiency. However, in light of changing demographics, socio-economic factors, and the influences of technology that have directly and indirectly affected the community, a new stewardship paradigm must be explored in order for the church to survive.

Notes

1. J. LaVon Kincaid, *God's Faithfulness: Stewardship in the Ethnic Minority Church* (Nashville: The United Methodist Publishing House, 1980), 27.

2. Herbert Mather, *Becoming a Giving Church* (Nashville: Discipleship Resources, 1992), 25.

Chapter Two

DEVELOPING A THEOLOGY OF GENEROSITY

*"Moreover, it is required of stewards that
they be found trustworthy."*

1 CORINTHIANS 4:2

G od calls us to be stewards. The word *steward* comes from the Greek word *oikonomos*, meaning a manager or caretaker of a household. The word *stewardship* is derived from the Greek word *oikonomia*, and from the word *epitropos*, meaning custodian or guardian. Being a manager or caretaker acknowledges that everything belongs to God (Psalm 24.1). When we recognize our possessions really belong to the Lord, we begin to feel God's call for believers to be generous.

It all begins with God's grace. We come into this world flawed and broken, but by grace we are restored. Grace is God's unique gift crafted for us, inwardly showering us with love and comforting mercy. Paul said, "For the grace of God has appeared, bringing salvation to all" (Titus 2:11). God showed us grace and generosity in Jesus Christ, who lived the model life, and died for the forgiveness and redemption of our sins. Out of God's grace, we are called to be generous.

It is God's unmerited gift of grace that makes us blessed. Grace cannot be purchased, nor earned. Further, it is something one cannot qualify. Because of God's grace, we receive God's anointing, blessing, guidance, power, protection, and provision. This is quite an assortment of gifts, all wrapped under God's grace. Paul appropriately quoted the Lord, "My grace is sufficient for you, for power is made perfect in weakness" (2 Corinthians 12:9). With a never exhausted, ever-giving gift of grace from a generous God, we have cause to be generous.

Being a generous Christian is not the same as being a frivolous or carefree spender or giver. Our generosity has purpose in God's plan for our personal lives, our corporate lives within God's church, and God's kingdom on earth. Funding mission and ministry in the local church and community takes financial resources. Making an impact and transforming lives requires resources. A community makeover necessitates significant funds. To do the work of the Lord engenders a spirit of generosity. We may not all possess the spiritual gift of generosity, but we can develop a heart of generosity.

Because of faith, we can loosen our reins on possessions. Faith is defined in Hebrews 11:1, as " . . . the assurance of things hoped for, the conviction of things not seen." Faith assures us of what is to come, and God's grace provides for the past and the present.

Jesus realized that we would have issues concerning money and possessions, and many of his parables and teaching dealt with these subjects. Over 2000 verses in the Bible touch the subject of money and possessions. The parable of the Rich Young Ruler in Matthew 19:16-30 is an excellent example of the struggle and stress caused by having significant financial resources. Persons of limited financial means are not immune from the same challenges as the rich young ruler. This parable is about a young man who asked Jesus, "What must I do to have eternal life?" The young man was a faithful believer, but he was too attached to his wealth and possessions. Jesus challenged the man's desire to have eternal life when he asked him to sell his possessions and give his money to the poor. The rich young ruler walked away when he heard this challenge. Jesus said to his disciples, "It is easier for a camel to go through the eye of a needle than for someone who is rich to enter the kingdom of God" (Matthew 19:24).

Each denomination or non-denominational fellowship has its own theological foundation or perspective relating to stewardship. Theological perspectives can be viewed as conservative, moderate, or liberal when it comes to giving. Within denominations, congregations and members will have varying views on the subject of stewardship.

The starting point of theological perspectives on giving covers the entire spectrum. Members of denominations and congregations from conservative theological perspectives have a tendency to give a higher percentage of their household income. Many embrace a literal or conservative interpretation of the Bible, and thus are more likely to adopt tithing as the foundation for biblical giving. Tithing is taught as the starting point for giving, and the offering is given after the tithe. High-expectation churches cover the gamut in theological perspectives, but more importantly, members are given a high threshold of expectation in giving, with the tithe usually being the minimum. These churches tend to have strong Christian education components.

The starting point for giving in moderate theologically based churches is usually not emphasized in the same manner as conservative churches, even though the tithe remains the benchmark for biblical giving. Proportionate giving is often emphasized as the place to begin, while the eventual goal is to reach the tithe. Tithing is taught, but the teachings within these denominations or churches are not as rigid as the theologically conservative churches and denominations or the high-expectation churches. Churches that practice a liberal theology, and do not emphasize the biblical standard of tithing, tend to underachieve in giving levels as compared to churches and denominations that embrace conservative and moderate theological perspectives.

Through theological and Christian education, theologies of generosity can develop. In the Bible, many parables and verses can help clergy and laity develop a theology of generosity. Choosing a parable or text to define and describe our understanding of stewardship requires more than a story or a sermon to inspire members to give more. The parable or passage should touch hearts and invite people to wrestle with questions such as:

How is it with my soul? What is my relationship with the Lord? What is important in my life? How do my actions reflect my priorities of faith? What are my responsibilities to others?

There are many stories to choose from, but there is usually one that touches the soul and transforms the heart. Eugene Grimm, in his book *Generous People*, encourages people to examine their lives and see God's generous hand.[1] Throughout the Bible, God's generosity is present. It was God who sent manna from heaven to the Hebrew people wandering in the wilderness. "Being a generous giver is a spiritual response to God's goodness."[2]

As pastor or layperson, articulating your theological understanding of generosity will help transform your congregation into a congregation of generous people. Examine your faith journey and search the scriptures for the parable or verse that will become part of your biblical foundation and theological framework for generosity. Prepare to pray, study, and seek the Lord's guidance in your development in becoming a generous giver. Some people base their understanding of giving on Leviticus 27:30, which establishes the tithe. The New Testament does not abolish the tithe as the biblical standard. While there is little reference to tithing in the New Testament, it does not suggest that we should give less to the Lord.

The believers in the early church, in chapter 2 of the Acts of the Apostles, shared *all* their possessions with one another. Others advocate for proportionate giving, which allows the giver to gradually reach the level of the tithe. Still, God calls us to the level of generosity. The use of biblical text allows believers to make the spiritual connection between faith and money.

Throughout the Bible, numerous passages and parables display the theme of generosity. Many of these parables and passages may be familiar to church people. They are the Bible stories and passages learned in Sunday school classes and Bible study. However familiar these stories may seem, many believers have not made a solid, spiritually grounded connection between faith and money. It is in the making of a connection between faith and money that we can begin to develop a mature theology of generosity. Consider the the following basics.

First, we recognize that God created everything. In Psalm 24:1, God's ownership and authority is established. "The earth is the Lord's and all that is in it, the world, and those who live in it." Understanding God's *ultimate* ownership of all possessions helps us move beyond materialism and toward good stewardship. Paul wrote in 1 Corinthians 4:2, "Moreover, it is required of stewards that they be trustworthy." Stewardship calls for

believers to be consistent in managing the resources God
has entrusted to us.

Second, in our theology of generosity and stewardship,
we must remember what Jesus said in Luke 10:27, "You
must love the Lord your God with all your heart, and with
all your soul, and all your strength, and with all your mind."
Here, we make our spiritual connection with the Lord and
all humankind. This connection allows us to think, feel, and
look beyond ourselves in all matters of life.

We must allow ourselves to embody the biblical principles of stewardship. Many people seem to practice a
principle of convenience and choice when it comes to the
Bible. Due to materialism and a consumerist society,
many omit scripture passages that would alter their
upscale lifestyles. God knew we would have issues
regarding money and possessions, so that is why this subject is discussed so often in the Bible. The Parable of the
Rich Fool (Luke 12:13-21) speaks of a man who made his
life's mission a matter of accumulating more and more, so
he built barn after barn to store his possessions. In the
parable Jesus said that God called the rich man a fool and
told him he couldn't take these things with him. I have
heard the same sentiment put another way, "There will
be no armored cars in your funeral procession." In Luke
12:21, Jesus spoke of those who store up treasures for

themselves, but are not rich toward God. Generosity begins with our gifts to the Lord and to the ministry and mission of the church.

Here are some other Bible stories to consider as we think about a theology of generosity.

The Widow's Offering

MARK 12:41-44

When it comes to significant expressions of generosity, the Widow's Offering should be one of the first Bible stories to come to mind. The widow's offering was more than generous; her gift was a sacrifice. She gave all that she had to the treasury. Her view of generosity was much different from the Rich Young Ruler or the Rich Fool, in Matthew 19:16-30 and Luke 12:13-21, respectively. Often, persons of limited means feel their small offerings do not matter. In truth, those contributions are special because of the spirit in which they are given. Those small gifts are great and powerful symbols of generosity. Jesus recognized the significance of the widow's gift because she gave all from her very limited resources. Others may have given more than the widow, but their gifts were lightweight tokens in comparison. The widow gave her best and her all. She demonstrated sacrifice. She gave all generations to follow her an awesome demonstration of her faith.

Your Heart

MATTHEW 6:19-21

God knows our hearts. God knows what we are passionate about and what we will support. In this text, Jesus warns his disciples about treasures–those things that are very important to us. The things we feel passion for are the things we support enthusiastically, consistently, and financially.

Examine your checkbook register. Let it show you what your treasures are. Look at your last credit card statement to see what your treasure is. Is that where your heart lies? Are the expenses recorded there your desired witness? Treasures are often determined by the frequency of our indulgence or participation. "For where your treasure is, there your heart will be also" (Matthew 6:21). We have many choices for our treasures. Is your treasure with God, mission, ministry, materialism, entertainment, or the accumulation of earthly wealth?

The Alabaster Jar

MARK 14:3-9

The story of the woman who anointed Jesus at Bethany is one of the most powerful stories of generosity in the Bible. This woman anointed Jesus with an expensive ointment. Aside from the story of the Widow's Offering, this woman probably gave proportionately the most significant gift. Her story illustrates generosity and sacrifice because she was a person of limited means. It should be noted that the ointment she placed on Jesus' feet was very costly, even for persons of significant means. The ointment of nard was valued over 300 denarii, which was close to a laborer's annual salary. Her peers chastised her for her good deed, because they felt the proceeds from the sale of the ointment would have better served the poor. Often, when we receive the spirit of generosity, our peers shun it. This woman gave out of her love for Jesus.

The power of this story lies behind how she opened the alabaster jar. Alabaster was often used because it was the most effective mineral in preserving ointments. In fact, it is a form of marble and must be broken in order to be opened. Therefore, once the jar was opened, she had to use it all. Our generous follower broke the container, which means she had no intentions of holding back or saving some of her expensive ointment for another occasion. She gave her best, and she gave her all!

The Macedonian Model

2 CORINTHIANS 8:1-15

This passage in 2 Corinthians is often referred to as the Macedonian Model, because of how Paul encourages and challenges the church at Corinth to emulate the Macedonian church's generosity. The Macedonian church was not an affluent body of believers, but they believed in strongly supporting ministry. The church at Corinth was the complete opposite. This church had persons of wealth, because Corinth was a prosperous commercial shipping center with a large population. Paul used this letter to stimulate and cultivate a culture of generosity in the church at Corinth. In this passage there are four demonstrations of generosity: first they gave voluntarily; secondly, they gave beyond their means; thirdly, they gave eagerly; and lastly, they gave their best.

Verse 15 gives us all words of encouragement, "The one who had much did not have too much, and the one who had little did not have too little." These very words can transform your practice of giving, and cultivate a new theology of generosity in your life as well as your congregation.

The Collection for the Saints

2 Corinthians 9:1-15

Throughout chapter 9 of Paul's second letter to the church at Corinth, he shares with the church how we should give. Here, we learn why God encourages us to become cheerful givers. Further, we discover the manner of giving that pleases God and empowers other communities of believers with resources for ministry and assistance.

Many pastors share messages that distort verse 6 of this text, "the one who sows sparingly will also reap sparingly, and the one who sows bountiful will also reap bountifully," encouraging their members to expect financial windfalls. Prosperity preachers and some televangelist preach messages to encourage persons to give and give, with the expectation of receiving a ten-fold or a one hundred-fold blessing. Often these ministers prey on the emotions of believers who can least afford to seed several gardens of different ministries. God rewards and blesses generous givers in a variety of ways, and financial windfalls are not necessary the only manner in which God blesses us.

It is important for us to recognize God cannot be manipulated with our gifts. Sowing seeds into the Lord's ministry is not akin to playing the lottery, hoping for a big payout, or investing in the stock market, with anticipation of receiving a great return a few days after a stock purchase. We cannot play "Let's Make a Deal" or "The Price is Right" with God. Our windfall or harvest from God often comes in the form of life transforming ministry.

What is most important about 2 Corinthians 9 is how Paul encourages people to give, and the importance of giving to those outside of the household of faith. When we become cheerful givers, we will begin to recognize God's generosity in our lives.

There are many passages of scripture in the Old and New Testaments that will help us develop a theology of generosity. I encourage you to pick a biblical story that will help you develop a deep spirit of generosity. As you read the Bible, be open and allow a passage to speak clearly to you and to your church concerning the theology of generosity. Pray for God's guidance and wisdom, and for obedience to allow God's word to transform you and give you a spirit of generosity.

Notes

1. Eugene Grimm, *Generous People: How to Encourage Vital Stewardship* (Nashville: Abingdon Press, 1992).

2. David Bell, General Board of Discipleship, *Healthy Church* Presentation, Houston, Texas.

Chapter Three

LEADERSHIP ROLES IN STEWARDSHIP

*"For God did not give us a spirit of
cowardice, but rather a spirit of power
and of love and of self-discipline."*

2 TIMOTHY 1:7

The role of leadership is vitally important in the life
of any organization. Often, leadership in the church
is pastor-centered, and sometimes the church depends
too much upon the pastor. However, the church consists
of many leaders. These leaders are not limited to persons
who hold office. Leaders are persons whom others
respect, and from whom they seek their guidance.
Leaders lead!

Pastoral leadership is necessary when discussing the development of a culture of generosity in congregations, but it is also important to have the involvement of active lay leadership. Remember that the church is an active partnership between clergy and laity, especially when developing a culture of generosity. Clergy and laity need each other in the undertaking of a stewardship paradigm shift. Leaders lead!

John C. Maxwell, a pastor and an authority on leadership, included the Law of E.F. Hutton when he wrote his book, *The 21 Irrefutable Laws of Leadership*.[1] Years ago the brokerage firm E.F. Hutton created many memorable television commercials that featured the motto, "When E. F. Hutton speaks, people listen." You may have seen these television commercials. The setting was typically a busy restaurant or other public place. Two people talked about financial matters, and the first person repeated something his broker had said concerning a certain investment. The second person said, "Well, my broker is E. F. Hutton, and E.F. Hutton says . . ." At that point everyone in the restaurant stopped, turned toward the speaker, and listened. Maxwell contends that when leaders speak, others listen. In many churches, the leaders are persons who do not hold office, but wield influence, and have "the E. F. Hutton effect" on others.

Many clergy are reluctant to talk or preach about money. They are uneasy partners in the task of teaching about stewardship. One reason for this neglect is that clergy compensation is derived from the tithes and offerings, so teaching and preaching about giving appears to be self-serving. Ministerial salaries are often hot-button issues in churches. Another reason may be the lingering feeling that how we use our money is material, not spiritual, and not a proper subject for teaching and preaching in a church setting. If teaching and preaching on stewardship intimidates clergy, then the role of leadership in stewardship almost becomes impossible. Don Joiner says, "Where the leaders lead, the congregation will follow."[2]

The church often avoids the topic of stewardship. Some clergy feel uncomfortable talking about stewardship because of a lack of training in that subject area. Laity are afraid of offending their peers when discussing money. Discussing stewardship can cause our peers to become defensive if they are underachievers in supporting the ministry of the church. Further, the subject challenges values and priorities both personal and spiritual. That is why it is imperative for clergy and laity to support each other as they implement a plan of stewardship for their congregation.

Clergy and laity share many fears about money. Listed below are fears of both clergy and laypersons, adapted from a 1994 study by Ronald Vallet:

1. The pastor is viewed as self-serving, seeking to raise money to pay his or her own salary.

2. There is already too much preaching and talk about money.

3. The pastor wants to avoid unpopular topics, so as to be liked.

4. If the pastor preaches about money, people may become angry, offended, or leave the church.

5. The pastor may feel a lack of sufficient knowledge to preach on the subject.

6. People think that money and possessions are unspiritual. Money is the responsibility of boards or committees, such as the trustees. The pastor is called to preach on spiritual matters, which do not include money. The connection between faith and attitudes about money is ignored or missed entirely.

7. Preaching about money is too personal; people resist changes in their personal lifestyles.

8. The pastor wants to avoid placing a financial burden on his or her people.

9. The pastor may not be giving what he or she knows should be given.

10. Preaching about money may not fit smoothly into the preaching schedule because other faith issues are viewed as more important.

11. Sermons about money create feelings of guilt.

12. Some people feel they already give all they can and struggle to pay their own bills.

13. The commitment of some people is shallow and does not include their money.

14. Some people think, "All they want is my money."

15. Some people do not like to have their preconceived ideas about money and stewardship challenged, and their excuses for not giving adequately to the church destroyed.[3]

Once church leaders renew themselves around personal issues of money, they will find courage and skill to improve their preaching and teaching about money.[4] In our society we have made money a private and personal matter. In reality, money is a spiritual matter that affects several facets of ones life. If money matters were private and personal, Jesus would not have allocated the amount of time he used teaching on the subject. Secularization and consumerism have made money a private and personal matter. In light of this shift, money has become a subject pastors and church leaders shy away from. Further, they steer away from the discussion of money in order to avoid the possibility of offending people or making them uncomfortable.

Combating Fear

Once pastors and laypersons address their fear of the spiritual matter of money, then open dialogue on that subject can be established and maintained. The best way for pastors and church leaders to combat their fear of discussing money is to always use the Bible. Members of the Body of Christ should not object to anyone using scripture to encourage them to support the mission and ministry of the church. I believe members are eager to learn what the Bible says about Christian stewardship. Through preaching, teaching, and giving testimonies, we can combat fears of discussing money in our congregations.

When or if members of the congregation intimidate the pastor or other leaders about discussing money, then the task of teaching stewardship becomes a challenge. As a pastor, I faced a number of challenges from officers of the church when I discussed stewardship practices such as tithing, stewardship sermon series, pledging, sacrificial offerings, capital campaigns, and endowments. Most churches usually resist the introduction of new ideas and concepts. Resistance usually comes in the form of negativity. Anxiety typically would escalate before acceptance of the new concept. A stewardship initiative like any new initiative is a process. In most cases, there is fear of the unknown, but in this case, fear centers on stepping up to biblical stewardship. For many, this requires officers and leaders of the church to increase their support of the church according to biblical teachings. Tithers or generous givers seldom resist biblical stewardship foundations and stewardship practices that will bless the church. Through prayer, teaching and perseverance, leaders can create a culture of generosity. Keeping a biblical perspective is imperative when trying to change the culture of giving in a congregation.

Often, church members underachieve when it comes to stewardship, so challenging the status quo is vitally important. It is through spiritual exercise and challenge that we grow in our faith. Challenge the core leadership regarding generosity through group Bible study before meetings. I encourage all finance committees to have Bible study or devotion as part of meetings, so they can remain spiritually fresh. Viewing church expenses and offerings can be overwhelming and challenging to the faithful, if the Word does not undergird the work.

Leaders lead! I firmly believe the pastor should have access to the giving records of the membership of the church. The pastor must openly demonstrate a spirit of generosity. Persons in leadership should generously support the church. It is difficult for leaders to lead where they have never gone or are afraid to venture. Too often, I hear pastors say, "I don't want to know who gives what, so I will not be tempted to treat them differently." That is usually a sign that they do not have access to records. More importantly, leaders can positively or negatively affect giving in congregations, because of their leadership roles. A leader known to give little towards the support of the church can adversely influence others to give little. Conversely, a generous person can positively influence others throughout a congregation to give generously. The widow in the story of the Widow's Mite has been a positive influence to other believers for centuries. Generosity is not measured in amounts, but in the spirit in which it is given. Leaders lead!

Develop a group of generous givers, so they will help promote a spirit of generosity throughout the congregation. Often, our generous members are bashful about discussing their generosity before the congregation because they are afraid of upsetting members or making them uncomfortable. I always encourage people who are given the responsibility of sharing stewardship before the congregation to hide behind the Bible, and allow God's Word to protect them. Remember the E.F. Hutton effect.

Notes

1. John C. Maxwell, *The 21 Irrefutable Laws of Leadership* (Nashville: Thomas Nelson Publishers, 1998), 45.

2. Donald W. Joiner, *Creating a Climate for Giving* (Nashville: Discipleship Resources, 2002), 14.

3. Ronald E. Vallet, *Congregations at the Crossroads* (Grand Rapids: Wm. B. Eerdmans Publishing Company, 1998), p. 53

4. Mark Vincent, *Speaking About Money: Reducing the Tension* (Scottdale, PA: Herald Press, 2001), 64.

Chapter Four

STEWARDSHIP IN A NEW ERA

"For everything there is a season . . . "

ECCLESIASTES 3:1

At the dawn of a new millennium, the church finds itself experiencing many socio-economic changes. For some reason or another, the church recognizes and responds to changes at a much slower pace than other areas of society. In the area of finance and stewardship, there are new practices in place that usher churches into doing stewardship in new ways. Church members have been exposed to these ideas at their secular jobs or in their daily lives, but never thought about how they might work in their church. For those who work in planning, operations, finance, and accounting, embracing these new practices comes quickly.

A Year-Round Approach

The new paradigm in stewardship consists of a year-round approach to stewardship. This approach breaks away from the old paradigm of dues, fundraisers, and special day offerings. A year-round approach helps reemphasize stewardship as a lifestyle.

Throughout the year stewardship needs to be preached, taught, and practiced. A year-round calendar should be implemented with strategically scheduled programs, events and activities. Some of the activities build on the Christian year. Other activities are performed monthly, quarterly and annually. Part of this year-round approach includes the ways in which we talk about money and celebrate giving as an act of worship, which funds ministry. This approach leads churches in creating a culture of generosity.

Being biblical, intentional, and strategic helps transform churches into places where stewardship becomes a way of life. Subsequent sections of this chapter discuss portions of a year-round calendar. The appendix includes a sample stewardship calendar that encompasses a year-round approach.

The Annual Appeal and Estimated Giving

All churches should celebrate a month when growing stewards is the primary focus. You may wish to call it "Stewardship Month" or "Financial Empowerment Month," but it's important to set aside an entire month and allow it to become an annual time to explore aspects of stewardship. Designating an entire month for stewardship emphasis declares that stewardship is an important facet of discipleship. The months of September, October, and January are excellent months for stewardship awareness. September and October work well because they precede Thanksgiving and Christmas, and it sets the tone for the coming year. January is also a great time for stewardship month because it is the beginning of a new year. As one colleague shared with me, the additional benefit of stewardship month taking place in January is that pledges may take into account pay increases. Many churches have annual revivals, homecomings, and anniversaries, often filled with a month of activities, so why not observe a month lifting up biblical stewardship?

Some pastors and church leaders believe that designating a month for stewardship causes members to miss church for the entire month, but this usually is not the case. Most believers want to learn more about being good stewards. During such a special time believers will learn that stewardship is more than about money; it is about a Christian lifestyle. Fill the stewardship month with opportunities to educate believers about biblical stewardship. Do not limit the focus to increased financial support of the ministry. Instead, focus on becoming better stewards of all that God has entrusted to us. During this month, expose the congregation to biblical teachings on personal debt, saving money, investing, and giving.

If you do not have a stewardship team or committee, create one separate from the finance committee. Encourage both groups to support the church's mission and ministry, while each utilizes different skill sets. People who effectively work on the finance committee are usually good at working with numbers and are detailed oriented, and that skill set is not as useful when working on the stewardship team. Many churches do not have a separate stewardship committee from the finance committee. If you do not have a separate stewardship team, create one. Doing so is an opportunity to develop new leaders and empower persons who are best gifted for the stewardship team or committee. Considered persons for the team who give faithfully, think creatively, and communicate well. The E. F. Hutton appeal helps. Normally, it takes three to four months to plan an effective annual stewardship appeal or stewardship month.

The stewardship team, together with the pastor, sets a calendar for planning sessions and dates for implementation and action. For the program to be a twelve-month success, select a biblically-based stewardship theme and support it by scripture and prayer. Present a vision for ministry and keep the vision before the congregation. The theme should be memorable and spiritual. That theme will become a quote members will grasp and hold onto for the next twelve months. "Keep it positive. Keep it biblical. Stress the mission."[1]

Warning! Pastors and laypersons often tell me that members will never pledge, but I disagree. I always encourage them to ask their leaders to raise their hands if they have a mortgage, a car note, or pay utility bills. If they raise their hands in response to any of those questions, help them realize each of these are pledges. The mortgage is usually for thirty years, the car note is typically for thirty-six to sixty months, and utilities go on as long as we are alive. After that is resolved, it becomes a matter of people making a commitment to the Lord's work. Pledgers tend to give more than non-pledgers.

People who pledge a percentage usually pledge more than those who pledge a dollar amount.

Plan activities for stewardship month, such as skits during the worship services, ministry moments given by ministry workers, and statements of support by faithful givers. I encourage pastors to plan a sermon series on several areas of stewardship, such as personal debt, saving, investing, and giving. Positive and intriguing sermon series titles provide a strong foundation for the annual stewardship appeal. Involve the whole church in a prayer ministry by constructing a schedule for members to take turns praying for mission and ministry. Designate a set time each day for members to pray during stewardship month. Consider having a weekend prayer vigil at the church and invite people to sign up for thirty minutes or an hour of prayer in the sanctuary or chapel.

Two weeks prior to the start of stewardship month, send a letter to every member or family in the congregation and announce the theme of the stewardship month. Include the scripture, sermon titles, special Bible study, and a pledge or an estimated giving card.

Begin the first Sunday of stewardship month with skits, ministry moments, and a statement of support of the vision and ministry of the church. Each of these will help emphasize the theme. These actives also allow for additional members to participate, and show open support for their church.

The most significant part of the annual appeal is the consecration of the estimated giving cards. Plan this event for worship on the last Sunday of the month. Invite the members to bring their cards to the chancel rail or place them on the altar. Officers and key leaders should bring their cards first, leading the way for the congregation. Remember that the cards symbolically represent our commitment. Those who come forward make a conscious decision to support the Lord's church. Make this part of the service special.

Send letters of thanks to those who submitted estimated giving cards. Express gratitude for their outward support of and confidence in the vision, mission, and ministry of the church. The finance committee should use the estimated total of the giving cards for strategic planning. Only the treasurer, financial secretary, and pastor will see the individual estimated giving cards.

Contribution Statements

Quarterly or monthly individual contribution statements are valuable informational tools. Finance committees and stewardship teams can use them to educate and inform members of the church. Countless pastors have proudly informed me, "We send out statements at the end of the year." Sadly, they have missed three additional opportunities to enhance stewardship. The contribution statement is more than just a statement; it is a great communication medium concerning commitment and ministry. I refer to it as a *"Statement of Celebration"*, because they celebrate the Lord's work.

These statements include a letter that allows the pastor and key leaders to communicate the vision of the church. The quarterly *Statement of Celebration* also celebrates joys of the church, shares scripture, discusses seasons of the Christian year, thanks members for their support, and informs contributors of the amount of their support for the previous quarter. Think about quarterly statements as a means of communicating and promoting stewardship in the life of the church.

As I consult with churches, people ask, "Why send these statements so often?" My response is always the same: MasterCard, Visa, Discover, and American Express send us reminders each month. They attempt to motivate us to purchase things we do not need. Our bank, credit union, or mortgage company provides us with a coupon book as a reminder of our debt, and we use these to receive proper credit for our payments. These friendly reminders represent a form of our commitment as well as a notice of our debts. I believe our contribution statements are simply a reminder of our commitment to God and the church, and the debt Jesus paid for us all.

Churches that send timely contribution statements usually experience consistent giving. The statements serve as individual barometers of stewardship. Persons who record individual contributions will notice changes in giving patters. Those patterns can indicate a spiritual issue, a disturbance with a church matter, a job change or unemployment, or major medical expenses. In any case, the pastor should be informed and plan to visit and comfort the family.

Summer months can be dreadful in large and small churches. Offerings often slump because of a decline in attendance due to vacations, weddings, and family reunions. During the first week of May, send a letter of encouragement to members and remind them to remember their church while they are on vacation. Send monthly statements for the summer, if necessary. Just tell them, "Remember God's church while you are on vacation. God does not take a vacation or a sabbatical. God still supplies all of our needs." These letters are well worth the postage.

Electronic Giving

We live in an age filled with high technology. Living in such times causes us to conduct business differently. Many of us now shop, pay bills, and bank online using our personal computers. For years, automatic drafts or electronic funds transfer have been used to take money from our checking accounts to pay car loans, insurance premiums, and home mortgages. Further, a large percentage of people have direct deposit of payroll and retirement checks into savings or retirement accounts.

Prayerfully consider offering the option of electronic giving to members in your church. Electronic giving or electronic transfer of funds (ETF) allows for a style of giving that has grown in popularity in our technological age. With anything new, there can be hesitancy and opposition when different practices or procedures are implemented. You are probably saying to yourself, or can picture someone saying, "We have never done it that way before." Move beyond those barriers.

Pastors and church leaders often struggle with the offering plate when discussing whether to offer electronic giving to their congregation. Some oppose electronic giving because they feel it does not seem consistent with biblical principles such as bringing the tithe into the storehouse or giving first fruits. Others will say, "Those who give electronically will not have anything to place in the offering plate on Sundays." For those who give electronically, provide a card or a stamp for them to place in an envelope, so they can symbolically give in worship along with the rest of the congregation.[2] The benefits of electronic giving (e-giving) outweigh any negative feelings. E-giving provides for first fruits giving, consistent giving, and predictable giving. Further, it allows for a more even cash flow during vacation periods and inclimate weather.

This option can be provided through an institution that specializes in offering this service. Often, a bank or the church can do it themselves. The information needed for setup includes: a record of member's permission, their bank account and bank routing numbers, the account holder's name, and the amount and date. Collect a voided check with the enrollment form to reduce data entry errors. Now you are ready to receive electronic gifts to support the ministry of your church.[3]

If you are interested in offering e-giving in your church, place a note in your Sunday bulletin asking, "If you are interested in supporting the ministry of your church through electronic giving, please contact the church office." This will allow the church to gauge the level of interest of persons who are interested in this option, without committing to implementing it right away.

E-giving may or may not be for your congregation today, but it is clearly a part of the technological age we live in. Electronic giving helps churches and individuals by making giving convenient, consistent, and accurate.[4]

New Members Class

A highlight for any congregation occurs when new members join the body of Christ. Receiving new converts or receiving members by transfer brings awesome responsibilities. Leading new converts to become faithful members requires intentional teaching. Most converts or transfers come to the community of faith excited and eager to learn what the church believes, and the responsibilities and expectations of each member.

New members of high-expectation churches attend a member's orientation class to help them become part of the church family. This class course is an excellent time to share biblical teachings on Christian discipleship. Devote a lesson or session to the topic of biblical giving. Share with the participants, from a biblical perspective, why we give (Malachi 3:8-10), how much we should give

(Leviticus 27:30), when we should give (1 Corinthians 16:2), and how we should give (2 Corinthians 9:7). Newly committed members of the Body of Christ will be more receptive and less resistant to a new paradigm of stewardship because they are eager to respond to the grace of God in Jesus Christ.

Often, these persons will become some of your most committed workers and supporters in your congregation. These members are new and do not live with engrained church traditions. Invite those who are converts or transfers to participate in a new member's class within a month of joining the church. This will prevent them from embracing other giving traditions of the church, such as fundraisers, or thinking that they should pay dues.

Narrative Budget/Narrative Spending Plan

The church puts together an annual budget that serves as a guide for fiscal spending within the given ministry areas in a church. Many of us are familiar with the line-item budget, which identifies by name ministry or expense areas. I find this type of budget boring, difficult to understand, and typically an inaccurate picture of the life and vision of our churches. Another financial guide is called the *narrative budget* or *spending plan*, which gives members a new and vivid picture of the ministries the church participates and supports.

A narrative spending plan or budget creates a financial story for the upcoming year that estimates the costs of accomplishing goals, and provides a plan for spending resources.[5] Moreover, it places more emphasis on ministry and mission. Dreams and visions may grow without being suffocated by a lack of faith and numbers crunching.

"Most of what is contained in a line-item budget is of little interest to the majority of people who attend our churches."[6] Too often the focus is aimed towards the pastor or pastoral staff's compensation package, administrative cost, and denominational support. Consider placing the focus on ministry. Instead of starting with the pastor's compensation package and administrative cost, place it at the end. This is not an attempt to hide or conceal anything; it is an effort to make ministry the main attraction.

A narrative budget or spending plan may come in a variety of forms. It should be creative and informative. Again, its purpose is to take the attention off numbers and shift it onto ministry. Include pictures and give an account of how a particular ministry area has made a difference in the life of the congregation, community, or some individual's life. Divide the narrative budget/ spending plan into at least four basic areas: Worship, Mission, Program, Pastor/Administrative Support, and Facilities/Maintenance.

Share the story of each area. If you expand or implement new ministries in the coming year, cast your vision for that new ministry and its proposed impact in the narrative budget/spending plan. This is a great opportunity to generate additional support for that particular ministry.

Why should you consider a narrative spending plan or budget? For many pastors and laypersons, reading and interpreting a line-item budget is a challenge, and it allows very little room for sharing the church's story and vision for ministry. A narrative-spending plan takes the focus off the crunching of numbers, and places it on the lives of persons who the ministry has touched. Not only does it take the focus off dollars and cents, but also it paints an accurate picture of where members' contributions go. Further, it helps connect the marginal attendee with the mission, ministry, and vision of the church. People who attend once or twice monthly often do not have a clear understanding of what their church does in the community, or how it touches lives. Reading a narrative-spending plan has the potential to transform a marginal attendee into a committed member. The resulting new discoveries of ministry may encourage them to become more active and more generous in supporting the ministry of the church.

The line-item budget and the narrative budget or spending plan can co-exist. Number crunchers prefer the line-item budget, but the majority of the church membership will embrace the narrative budget or spending plan. Form a group of people from the programming and finance committee, along with someone who is gifted in writing and desktop publishing. You will see that the narrative budget-spending plan will have an impact on your congregation, both spiritually and financially.

Using Preprinted Offering Envelopes

Consider using personal, preprinted offering envelopes. There are envelope companies that offer many services with a variety of benefits.

Congregations that utilize this type of service typically receive preprinted envelopes in the mail on a quarterly basis. The envelopes provide each giver with the convenience of writing his or her check or placing cash in the envelope prior to arriving for worship. The envelopes serve as a reminder of commitment to ministry.

Further, the assigned numbers help keep accurate records of contributions.

When considering implementing a service utilizing individual preprinted offering envelops, it is important to test the feasibility of the service. Also, determine whether it fits the personality of your membership.

Year-end Giving and Other Matters

The end of the year presents additional opportunities for believers to give. Towards the end of the year, Christians should reflect on how the Lord has blessed them during the year. During this time of reflection, members will recognize blessings that may have resulted in financial windfalls. Churches need to challenge members to consider year-end gifts and other types of giving.

Members in our congregations receive stock options from their employers. Others invest in the stock market as a means of saving and accumulating wealth. Seniors who have retirement accounts may want to make year-end gifts to the church, if those resources are not needed to supplement retirement income. At age seventy and one-half, holders of individual retirement accounts must make mandatory withdrawals. For some persons, investment accounts and individual retirement accounts are resources that they do not depend on for daily support, thus, these accounts remain in an accumulation mode. Each resource that I have mentioned is a source for year-end gifts that could be used to enhance ministry.

Christians are called to be good and faithful stewards. Stewards are encouraged to give out of duty, responsibility, and gratitude to the Lord. However, there are reasons why Christians give. Some give in order to reduce income tax liabilities. Even so, their gifts support ministry.

In September, place an insert or brochures that discuss year-end giving opportunities in the bulletin. Be prepared to assist donors in making their gifts by opening a brokerage account to receive securities, such as stocks and bonds. Advise donors to seek counsel with regard to tax implications associated with making donations.

Lastly, there are others types of gifts such as property, oil and gas leases or royalties, timber, antiques and other valuables that could be given as gifts to the church. Caution should be used in accepting any gift. A gift acceptance policy needs to be in place that will guide the church in gift acceptance, and protect it from receiving assets with liabilities or lengthy liquidations. (For further information about endowments and directed donations, see *Creative Giving* by Michael Reeves, Rob Fairly, and Sanford Coon.)

Remember, "From everyone to whom much has been given, much will be required; and from the one to whom much has been entrusted, even more will be demanded" (Luke 12:48).

Notes

1. Eugene Grimm, *Generous People: How to Encourage Vital Stewardship* (Nashville: Abingdon Press, 1992), 21.

2. Almetha Thomas, "E-Giving: Has Its Time Come for the Church?" (African-American Pulpit Digest, Summer 2002, Judson Press, Valley Forge, PA).

3. Matt Whitaker, "Is EFT Right for ME?" (Your Church Magazine, September/October 2004.

4. Almetha Thomas, "E-Giving: Has Its Time Come for the Church?" (African-American Pulpit Digest, Summer 2002, Judson Press, Valley, Forge, PA).

5. Mark L Vincent, *Speaking About Money: Reducing the Tension* (Scottdale, PA: Herald Press, 2001).

6. Dan R. Dick, *Revolutionizing Christian Stewardship for the 21st Century: lessons from Copernicus* (Nashville: Discipleship Resources, 2002), 93.

Chapter Five

STEWARDSHIP EDUCATION

*"My people are destroyed for lack
of knowledge . . . "*

HOSEA 4:6

The late Dr. Jonathan Jackson, Professor of Christian Education at The Interdenominational Theological Center in Atlanta, Georgia, would tell his students, "Christian education is the ministry that undergirds all of the ministries of the church."[1] Dr. Jackson profoundly shared his view of the importance of Christian education in providing the foundation for ministry throughout the church. Any church that desires to increase stewardship awareness must do so with stewardship education. This must take place at all levels, from children to adults, and attendees to officers. Moreover, it needs to be integrated into Sunday school, committee meetings, Bible study, and the preached word.

Many of our churches are not as strong in Christian education as was the case in earlier generations. If that trend is going to change, churches need to approach the issue intentionally and proactively. Attending a regular Bible study should be a requirement for leaders and members. Making paradigm shifts in churches to necessitate the implementation of a comprehensive stewardship education plan calls for education, imagination, and creativity. "Effective stewardship education always focuses on the need of the giver to give, not on the need of the church to receive."[2] Here are some ways to focus the ministry of Christian education on stewardship.

Bible Study

Bible study is an integral part of Christian discipleship. If transformation in the area of stewardship is to be sustained in our churches, then the process will start with Bible study. Because study of the Bible is a pillar for believers, study of God's word is essential. Through Bible study, Christians grow in faith and develop as stewards.

The traditional Wednesday night Bible study is a great place to begin integrating stewardship into the life of the church. Conducting a stewardship Bible study series once or twice a year will establish the importance of stewardship, but stewardship should not be left for only one discussion or conversation during the year. Remember that the majority of Jesus' parables dealt with money and possessions. Therefore, a stewardship Bible study series would fall in line with Jesus' teachings and the church's role in the world. Lead a study with lessons covering saving (Proverbs 21:5, 6:6-8), investing (Ecclesiastes 11:2, 5:13-14), greed (Matthew 6:24, Luke 12:13-21), and debt (Proverbs 22:7). Many Christian finance educators advocate a 10-10-80 plan, which calls for believers to give the Lord a tithe (ten percent), save ten percent, and live off the remaining eighty percent. It is important for believers to understand stewardship is more than giving to support the ministries of the church. When Christians discover their need to give grows out of a lifestyle of stewardship, the church will be the likely recipient of that generosity.

Create a lesson that encourages participants to further study the topic. Help people develop a lifestyle of stewardship by helping them with practical application.

Bible studies that teach, touch, and transform will develop faithful, generous disciples. Stewardship is part of a healthy church's discipleship-building regimen.

In churches where Bible study and church school have been anemic, it is crucial to recruit and train people to lead or facilitate studies in the area of stewardship. In many churches, the most consistent and faithful supporters are older adults who are going home to glory! There is an urgent need to develop our next generation of generous believers. Be intentional about offering stewardship related courses, and be assertive in encouraging members to attend those classes. It is imperative to stress the importance of the classes, and to strongly encourage members to attend those classes. "If believers are not taught . . . stewardship, can they be expected to give intelligently and can they be expected to realize that giving is indeed as vital a spiritual ministry."[3] Through the study of God's word, we become faithful, consistent, and generous givers.

Christian Finance

Churches and denominations across the country are faced with a crisis that stems from a culture that feeds into a society of instant gratification. The end result of these trappings is excessive consumer debt. Credit card debt causes financial paralysis. Many families are caught in a trap of paying only credit card minimum payments and feel that there is no way out. And if people pay only the minimum payment, there is no way out!

The church needs to step up and rescue its members from the spiritual warfare of consumerism and materialism. Being rescued from the trappings of excessive consumerism requires an understanding of contentment, defined by Paul in Philippians 4:11, "I have learned to be content with whatever I have." The church cannot bail people out of their financial debt, but it can teach people to use credit wisely and to think about or discern whether their purchases are wants or needs. Too often, individuals, couples, and families use credit cards to live beyond their means or upgrade their lifestyles. Strained finances streess family relationships.

Our churches need to offer Christian finance courses to members and to the community. Several good programs are available to help churches educate families about finances. The *Good $ense Ministry Program*, developed by Dick Towner and published by Willow Creek Church, is an excellent program that comes from a moderate theological perspective. The entire study can be taught in seven hours. Other financial education programs offered are: *Crown Ministry*, *Financial Peace*

University, and *Three Simple Rules*. *Crown* and *Financial Peace* come from a conservative theological view, and both courses last for thirteen weeks. *Three Simple Rules* is a good, brief course that centers on three basic rules, which help persons become good stewards. There is limited use of scripture in the course. You can go to their web sites to receive additional information at: good-senseministry.com, crown.org, daveramsey.com (Financial Peace University), and ThreeRules.com.

I encourage churches to offer family financial education courses at least twice a year. October and January are probably the best months to offer courses, because one precedes Christmas sales advertisements, and the other comes after Christmas and could help persons with consumer issues for the new year.

Christian finance courses not only address issues of debt, but also saving, investing, and giving. If our churches begin to assist members in addressing consumer debt, the church will become the ultimate beneficiary, because church members will spend quality time with their families, attend Bible study regularly, and serve in ministry due to a reduced need for additional employment and overtime. More importantly, a good Christian finance course will help people develop a lifestyle of stewardship, which is part of Christian discipleship.

Promoting Stewardship

Placing emphasis on stewardship should not be limited to Bible study, a Christian finance course, a sermon series, or stewardship emphasis month. Transforming a culture or making a paradigm shift requires a promotional plan that keeps stewardship before the congregation. The messages do not have to be heavy handed in order to be effective. They also must be consistent and constant.

There are several ways to promote stewardship without making it sound as if your church is struggling financially, or sounding like a prosperity-teaching congregation. It is important for members to be receptive to the subliminal messages of generosity. Here are a few ideas to promote stewardship as a lifestyle.

Every Sunday, members receive a bulletin that includes the order of worship. Consider creating bulletin inserts with a stewardship message. If your bulletin has several announcements, include a brief passage of scripture or a quote that speaks on money, possessions, or generosity. Designate a section of the bulletin for stewardship, and place material in that section weekly. Occasionally, share ministry joys so the congregation will see how their gifts make a difference in the lives of others.

Many churches have developed mission and vision statements. Why not have a stewardship statement? This statement is what the congregation believes or is striving towards. Your statement should be recited in unison at least once a month. Further, it should be placed in prominent places throughout the church, just as the vision and mission statements.

Newsletters are an excellent source of communication for congregations. Most newsletters consist of news and ministry highlights, a letter from the pastor, a calendar of events, and maybe a financial report. Effective newsletters also included sections for spiritual matters, which stewardship falls within.

Create a section in the newsletter for stewardship information. Name the section "Stewardship Seeds" or "Time, Talents, Gifts, and Service." Include scripture-based articles that cover how, why, when, where, and how much should be given. Reinforce the narrative budget plan by highlighting aspects of it. Connect stewardship with the Christian seasons of the church. Advent and Lenten season articles, written from a stewardship viewpoint, provide excellent teaching moments. For example, the magi exercised a form of stewardship and generosity when they visited the baby Jesus. The innkeeper and the shepherds also practiced forms of stewardship at the birth of Jesus.

Provide informational brochures for members to read on stewardship, particularly relating to areas of stewardship that are normally not discussed from the pulpit or in other ministry settings. Purchase or create personalized brochures that can be placed in the narthex, foyer, or informational center. These brochures may cover memorials, planned giving, year-end gifts, tithing, or proportionate giving. This gives members opportunities to discover additional ways of supporting the ministry of the church, and ideas as to how to support the church through biblical giving.

If brochures are not exciting enough, challenge youth and young adults in the church to create a video that highlights the story of the church's ministry. They might focus on a mission project faraway, or on a local shelter. Use the video to show why these ministries are important, as well as explain where the money goes to support these ministries.

If you are attempting to change the culture of your church or assist it in making a paradigm shift towards biblical stewardship, promotion is vital. By promoting stewardship, congregations encourage members to develop a lifestyle of stewardship and become generous givers. Stewardship education builds faithful, generous givers. Build them up with sound biblical teachings.

Remember, "My people are destroyed for lack of knowledge" (Hosea 4:6).

Notes

1. Jonathan Jackson, Class Lectures at the Interdenominational Theological Center, Atlanta, GA.

2. Eugene Grimm, *Generous People: How to Encourage Vital Stewardship* (Nashville: Abingdon Press, 1992), 39.

3. Stephen Olford, *The Grace of Giving: Message on Stewardship* (Grand Rapids, MI: Baker Book House, 1972), 14.

Chapter Six

CELEBRATING THE OFFERING

"Each of you must give as you have made up your mind. . . for God loves a cheerful giver."

2 CORINTHIANS 9:7

Today, the offering has almost become a perfunctory part of the worship service. However, the offertory is more than a time to collect money. The offering is an awesome act of worship unto the Lord. The presentation of God's tithes and offerings should be a time of great celebration. Giving in response to God's grace is cause for all Christians to give enthusiastically and cheerfully.

Over the years, the offering seems to have become an obstacle to the flow of worship in many churches. Some feel that it takes away from the singing and preaching. Others think the offering has little to do with worship and more to do with paying bills. They do not understand that *giving* is an act of worship. Sadly, it is not perceived as an act of worship because Christians are not taught to view the offering as worship. Worse yet, most churches do not plan the offertory.

I encourage pastors and worship committees to spend time planning the order of worship. These planning sessions should review the content of the service and the unity of the musical selections, the Bible readings, and the sermon. Invite the committee to consider how to introduce the offering.

There are many ways in which congregations can put excitement and celebration into the offering. Once we overcome our reservations to talking about money before the congregation, then we can begin to celebrate the offering. Throughout the worship services there are opportunities to talk about our response to God's generosity.

The creation of an environment for celebrating the offering comes through teachable moments in the worship service. Open the service with a call to worship that centers on stewardship as a part of discipleship. This will allow believers to see the connection between faith and money. The pattern of call and response of the call to worship establishes and sets the tone for the service. Moreover, the call to worship and the use of litanies allow Christian to see stewardship as being more than about money—it is a lifestyle that includes worship.

Music and singing have always been an integral part of worship. Use hymns and gospel selections that lift up giving and stewardship. The lyrics of hymns like, "You Can't Beat God Giving", "The Lord is Blessing Me Right Now", "He Has Done Great Things for Me", "Give of Your Best to the Master", and "What Shall I Render", possess deep theological meaning, which help us to understand more about our faith and God's grace.

Reading scripture on the topic of stewardship or leading meditations before the offering is vital to creating an environment for celebrating the offering. These meditations or passages of scripture create a biblical and theological framework for giving. These readings contain information on why, how, when, and the amount we should give to honor the Lord and support the church.

Our tithes and offerings support the ministry and mission of the church. Therefore, provide ministry moments given by laypersons who can articulate the correlation of faith, money, and ministry. Share stories with the congregation on the use of their gifts that will in turn transforms lives in the life of the church and the community.

Testimonies about tithing during the worship service provide listeners with a fresh perspective on giving patterns, generosity, and inspirations. Through personal reflection, the giver of the testimony can stretch and grow in his or her generosity. Those hearing testimonies are often inspired or encouraged by the witness of their brother or sister in Christ. The testimony giver and the person in the pew typically have both struggled towards generosity in their spiritual journey.

Preachers preach the word with great conviction. Do not apologize for what the Bible says about honoring the Lord with your gifts. Sprinkle your message with humor. Share insights on current trends in society, and how Christians can overcome the challenges of pitfalls. Preach one stewardship sermon each quarter of the year.

Finally, we get to the offering. For me, the offering is a special part of the worship service because we can all actively participate in this act of worship. Early in my ministry, the offertory time was somewhat filled with anxiety. I recall standing in the pulpit, repeating what I had heard for years, "Now it's time for the offering."

Those words felt empty as I saw the ushers come forward to receive the offertory plates. They walked toward the chancel rail as if they worked for Brinks or another armed security firm. They did not smile. We had no expressions of joy. Then I remembered that the Bible said, "Be a cheerful giver," and we began to change.

The offering must be planned, covered in prayer, and there must be anticipation of blessings from God. The offering is an act of worship, and our gift is an extension of ourselves. What we give is given out of our gratitude for what the Lord has done for us. That in itself should be enough cause to celebrate.

Boldly announce, "It's time to celebrate through giving." Read a passage of scripture that speaks of God's generosity, a biblical character's generosity, Jesus' parables on money and possessions, Paul's teachings on supporting the ministry of the church, or an offering meditation. Pray after the reading, and call the ushers to assist in receiving of the offering. Encourage the choir to sing an upbeat song that centers on giving or God's generosity, or ask the musicians to play "traveling music." Receive the offering from the ushers and lift it high as the doxology is sung. "In some ways, our gift to the church is the highest and most concrete act of worship we perform, simply because it is the most difficult; it requires us to sacrifice the work of our hand, the first of our labors, a good part of the legal tender with which we might otherwise have purchased many of the good things of life."[1]

Celebrating the offering means to worship the Lord with gladness as we come into God's gates with thanksgiving in our hearts. The Bible tells us we should not come empty handed. Our celebration displays our gratitude for God's generosity, protection, and provision. Truly, that is something all believers should enthusiastically celebrate.

Notes

1. Allan J. Weenink, *Proven Resources for Stewardship Promotion* (Lima, OH: CSS Publishing Company, 2001), 115.

Chapter Seven

WHAT TO DO WITH SPECIAL DAYS?

"And no one puts new wine into old wine-skins; otherwise, the wine will burst the skins, and the wine is lost . . . "

MARK 2:22

African-American churches celebrate special days. Celebrating special days like Church Anniversary, Homecoming, Women's Day, Men's Day, and more, are part of our heritage as the African-American church. These special days have historically been part celebration and part fundraiser. Often, large offerings are received on these days. I commend the special day celebration. I am,

79

however, not a big advocate of the fundraising aspect of special days. These special days often compromise biblical, regular, and systematic giving.

A significant number of people eagerly support special day requests, but fail to adequately support the church with consistent contributions throughout the year. Such practices deviate from biblical teachings like tithing, first fruits giving, and contributions based on prosperity. Special day offerings have a tendency to develop members who give mainly in response to special events requests. Hence, they fail to create a culture of generosity.

Further, these special offerings often fail to achieve financial goals. In some churches, due to falling membership or stagnant stewardship practices, special offerings income dwindles, or the special offerings cover a smaller percentage of the total operation budget. Moreover, the special offering requests for many congregations have remained the same for the last several years, without increases to compensate for inflation. A dollar of ten or twenty years ago does not possess the same value as a dollar today. According to the Consumer Price Index Inflation calculations, a $1.00 in 1980 and 1990 has the same buying power as $2.36 and $1.49, respectively in 2005. Therefore, financial shortfalls occur if a church does not have a significant number of tithers or proportionate givers who adequately support the ministry of the church. Relying upon special day offerings may force churches to add additional special days to make up financial shortfalls, which does not seem consistent with the biblical approach to stewardship known as tithing. Further, heavy reliance on these offerings often creates significant peaks and valleys in income for the church throughout the year. This can cause undue stress and anxiety for the pastor and leaders of the church.

I do not suggest the abolishment of special days, but encourage pastors and church leaders to educate and motivate members to give from a biblical perspective. When church members begin to respond with gratitude and joy to God's grace and generosity, then there is little need for an extraordinarily large offering on special days. We may then celebrate the purpose of each special day without worrying about whether we meet the budget. Special day offerings should be gifts beyond our tithe or regular giving. In fact, we should designate offerings on special days for projects and ministries outside of the operational budget.

I firmly believe special offerings should be designated for special projects and ministries opportunities. In the Old Testament, there were a number of offerings that were given after the tithe was presented. Those offerings supported special causes, such as meeting the needs of widows and orphans. Likewise, special day offerings should be considered over and above our regular giving, and should be designated for special projects and ministry opportunities.

Churches that preach, teach, and promote Christian stewardship year-round are less dependent on special offerings, compared to those that do not. These churches create an environment that promotes generosity and consistent giving. As disciples grow in their understanding of stewardship, church members will also look at special days from a different perspective. Many of these churches focus on reflecting on the past, celebrating the present, and anticipating the future. A vision for the future is a spiritual driving force that inspires these churches to be faithful in their response to the God's mission for the church. This Olan Hendrix quote states it best:

> Where there is no vision,
> The people perish.
> Where there is no plan,
> The vision perishes.
> Where there is no Stewardship,
> The plan perishes.[1]

Once your congregation begins to establish a culture of generosity, there will be many opportunities for celebration. Consider having a catered banquet or luncheon where every member can celebrate the life and ministry of the church. How would a pastor or a congregation know when their church has reached a place of generosity? It varies from church to church, but the commonality centers on disciple building and the openness to discussing stewardship as a means to actively serve in ministry. Members in these churches are eager to serve and fund ministry that will have an impact on lives and fulfill the mission of the church.

"Stewardship is a process, not an event."[2] It may take a few seasons before your special day celebrations to become a day of great celebration of ministry. Over time, your special day will become even more special because the focus will be on the reflection and celebration of ministry, and not on raising money.

Notes

1. Olan Hendrix, President of Leadership Resources Group (quoted from "Speaking About Money: Reducing the Tension" Scottsdale, PA, 2001), 9.
2. Michael Reeves, Texas Methodist Foundation material.

Chapter Eight

LEAVING A LEGACY

*"For we brought nothing into this world, so
that we can take nothing out of it . . . "*

1 TIMOTHY 6:7

Does your church have a permanent endowment fund? All churches large and small should establish a permanent endowment fund. The fund will help ensure ministry for the generations to come. It also allows members of the body of Christ to make a statement about their faith, their relationship with the Lord, and the church.

2 Chronicles 5:1 records the first endowment. Solomon placed the riches of his father, King David, in the Temple. Solomon did this to honor the Lord and to

sustain the Temple. Many of us have the same opportunity as Solomon—to give from our estate to our church's permanent endowment fund. We may not have the financial resources of David and Solomon, but God has blessed us with resources. David and Solomon left a legacy. You and I will each leave a legacy. How might we begin to think about the legacy that we leave behind? A legacy is much more than a gift to our church at our passing. It is part of our spiritual journey

What will be your legacy? Your legacy is more than accumulated assets. It is a statement of faith and belief; it is a statement of love. A legacy supports and sustains ministry after we have gone on to glory. Further, it is a way of showing our gratitude to the Lord, and to the church, which embraced, nurtured, and supported you throughout your life.

Your gift to the permanent endowment fund of your church can be given through your estate. I encourage all believers to prayerfully consider tithing their estate to the permanent endowment fund of the church. Assign a portion of a life insurance policy, declare your church sole beneficiary of a life insurance policy, or make a charitable gift annuity with the church being the beneficiary. Consider making your church a beneficiary of a retirement plan.

When establishing the fund, it is important to have specific instructions on the use and allocation of those funds. There should also be rules for amending the fund in the case the fund's goals change. Avoid using the principle or corpus of the fund. It is wise to allow your fund to grow to a designated amount before taking any withdrawals. The income generated by a fund with $50,000 will not produce the same amount as a fund with $100,000 or $250,000.

Permanent Endowments are not difficult to establish, but they require professional services. Some denominations have a foundation or professional staff that works with churches in establishing these funds. They will typically guide a church through the entire process, which includes legal documents, by-laws, structure, responsibilities, and legal requirements. If your church is not part of a denomination with a foundation, a local bank with a trust department will be able to serve and advise the church through the process.

The fund provides resources for special ministry projects, scholarships, and building maintenance beyond the operating budget. Some churches establish more than one fund, but in most cases it is not necessary. Churches with one fund most often distribute funds allocated to designated areas based on a predetermined percentage.

I do not encourage churches to depend on income from the fund to supplement the tithes and offerings of the church. The practice of using income from the permanent endowment fund to support the operational budget will handicap the members of the church. It will create a level of dependency that will undermine the development of a culture of generosity. Members will likely become underachievers in regard to biblical giving.

Permanent endowment funds are typically funded with gifts through deceased members' estates. Some are funded with other planned giving instruments, such as charitable gift annuities, charitable remainder trusts, and life estates. These instruments are more complex and require a professional to establish one for a donor.

There is another drawback to permanent endowments. Occasionally, I have discovered members making contributions to the fund when they are upset with the pastor or with the direction in which the church is going. This is clearly not the way the endowment is intended to be funded. Endowments are normally funded through accumulated resources and estates, not from current income. This is why gifts to endowments are often called legacy gifts.

Memorials are also an excellent way to provide resources for the endowment or special ministry projects.

Churches that receive memorials promote memorial gifts. Typically, a sub-committee of the endowment will promote memorial gifts by producing a brochure on how to make memorial gifts and how one can make a gift in memory of a loved one. Place the brochures in a highly visible area of the church. Share with the congregation the blessings and benefits of making memorial gifts in memory of a loved one. Send thank you notes to donors, and notes to family members. Place memorial gift information in a newsletter or church bulletin without the amount given. Memorials often range from $15 to $100. All Saint's Day (First Sunday in November) and birthdays are times when most memorials are given. Also, encourage members to make memorial gifts in lieu of flowers for funeral services. I often tell members, "Flowers wither away, but memorials keep living and giving."

Promoting the fund is vitally important in order to provide resources for future ministry. Many congregations have permanent endowments, but few actively promote the fund. Discussion of subjects related to death is difficult for most people, and the issue of money makes the discussion even more difficult. The problem with promoting the permanent endowment primarily centers on five challenges: the willingness to discuss monetary matters, difficulty in finding person who will passionately promote the fund, adequate training, working with potential donors, and funding the work of the endowment committee itself.

After establishing the fund, celebrate Endowment Sunday. As part of the celebration, create a special brochure to discuss the purpose of the fund and how people can contribute to the fund. The focus of the sermon and service should center on the fund and how it will bless the ministry of the church, and encourage the congregation to make a special gift to seed the fund. This should become an annual event in the life of the congregation. There is no special time of the year to have Endowment Sunday, but be mindful of the Christian calendar seasons and your current calendar. You will want to make this a special annual event in the life of your congregation.

To make planned giving a part of the culture of a congregation, there must a year-round plan for educating members about how they may make gifts that will last long after their lives. Place endowment brochures in the narthex or in the information center of the church. Use planned giving quotes in the worship bulletin, and place articles in the newsletter. Schedule wills and bequests seminars once or twice a year. Present a seminar called *Putting Your House in Order,* which prepares people for matters such as: estate planning, burial plans, living wills, the gathering of all personal financial information, and insurance policies. Invite attorneys, planned giving insurance agents, and funeral home directors to give seminars about wills and bequests, planned gifts, insurance policies, and burial plans. Many of these professionals will give these seminars without charge.

Encourage members to remember family, friends, and loved ones each year on All Saints Day with a memorial gift. Dedicating an entire month to this topic will help integrate legacy and planned gifts into the life of a congregation.

CONCLUSION

Today, we find ourselves in a new era where, "This is the way we have always done it," is no longer effective. Society has changed. The economy has change. Therefore, the church must make changes, too. The church is in a period of transition in many areas, including technology, accountability, and strategic planning, just to name a few. Accordingly, the church needs a paradigm shift for it to remain relevant and viable to the communities it serves. These shifts in thought must be transitioned in the spirit of Christ. Many of the ideas shared in this book will work in both small and large congregations. It is my prayer that this book will help you and your congregation make a paradigm shift to biblical stewardship.

Together, pastors and laypersons can make this shift happen and develop a culture of generosity in their congregations. The future of the church is bright with opportunities to engage in ministry like never before. When we develop a culture of generosity, mission and ministry will flourish and thrive. There will be enough resources to fund current ministries, as well as expand and create new ones.

Remember: Leaders lead! Lead believers to a place where generous people worship and serve with enthusiastic hearts. Remember to teach, preach, and celebrate stewardship as Christ taught his disciples.

APPENDIXES

CONGREGATIONAL STEWARDSHIP ANALYSIS

1. What is your church membership?

2. List your congregation's membership gains and losses during the last three years.

3. What is your current average worship attendance?

4. How many households does your church have?

5. How many contributing household giving units does your church have?

6. How many household units contributed at least $1,200 per year? Determine the age range of these contributors, breaking them down as follows: 20-39, 40-54, 55-69, and 70 plus.

7. Estimate the number of tithing household units in your congregation. What age brackets do these

household units fall within (20-39, 40-54, 55-69, and 70 plus)?

8. What is your current budget? The previous two years budgets?

9. What was your church income for the past three years?

10. Does your church have special offering appeals (i.e., Men's and Women's Day, anniversaries)? If so, how many, when, and how much does each raise?

11. Does your church have debt? If so, what is the amount of the debt, and what is the monthly payment?

12. Does your church conduct an annual pledge campaign? If so, when, and how many signed estimated giving cards are turned in?

13. Does your church issue monthly or quarterly contribution statements?

14. Does your church offer a Christian financial management course?

15. How many stewardship sermons did the congregation hear last year hear?

After retrieving this information, the finance and stewardship committees should meet to discuss the findings and propose a plan for improvements. This will require a series of meetings to accomplish this task. Identify the leading issues and draft a proposed plan. Present the plan to the governing board of the church for approval and implementation.

BIBLE STUDY

Bible study is a vital part of disciple building. Whether it is a personal or group study, we must ask the questions that invite us to grow spiritually.

General Format

Invite members of the study group to share something they have experienced during the week that was positive. The size or the magnitude of the event or blessing does not matter. The goal is to help believers feel comfortable sharing their stories and testimonies with others. Testimonies and witness often develop in these study groups and become a source of inspiration. You may use the following outline:

Open with prayer.

Introduce the background of the text.

Read the text.

Explore the text and develop questions for group discussion.

Practical Application: What is God saying to me through this study?

Closing close with prayer.

Bible Study I

Where Your Treasure Is . . .

BACKGROUND

Jesus was always concerned with society's thoughts and preoccupation with money and possessions, so he shared these thoughts with his disciples. His was primarily concerned about attachment to material possessions interfering with their quest for eternal life.

TEXT: MATTHEW 6:19-21

> *"Do not store up for yourselves treasures on earth, where moth and rust consume and where thieves break in and steal; but store up for yourselves treasures in heaven, where neither moth nor rust consumes and where thieves do not break in and steal.*

For where your treasure is, there your heart will be also."

1. What is the Lord saying to us, as it pertains to stewardship?

2. How does this text apply to us today? How does this text fail to apply to our lives?

3. What are the societal challenges of adhering to this passage of scripture? Are you faced with personal challenges of consumerism and materialism?

4. What do you treasure? Where is the evidence that you treasure that?

5. How do we apply principles from this text to our lives?

CONCLUSION

Jesus shared this passage of scripture with his disciples and others to help them understand that life is more than the accumulation of material goods. Examine your life to discover those things you treasure, so that you may make adjustments and prioritize your life. When we invest in the kingdom of God, the rate of return is greater and the eternal yield is substantially higher. Eternal investments are consistent and constant. Moreover, they never go out of style, there is never a market decline, never a sell off of shares, and with each deposit our balance appreciates with heavenly rewards. Plus, we accrue earthly blessings.

Bible Study II

The Master vs. MasterCard

BACKGROUND

This text is preceded by the parable of The Unfaithful Manager, who squandered the owner's resources and was discharged after the owner asked him to give an account of his work. Later, he collected outstanding debt for his former employer's clients, and presented them to his former employer. The owner commended the unfaithful manager for the unethical collection of his employer's money.

TEXT: LUKE 16:10-13

> *"Whoever is faithful in a very little is faithful also in much; and whoever is dishonest in a very little is dishonest also in much. If then you have not been faithful with the dishonest wealth, who will entrust to you the true*

riches? And if you have not been faithful with what belongs to another, who will give you what is your own? No slave can serve two masters; for a slave will either hate the one and love the other, or be devoted to the one and despise the other. You cannot serve God and wealth."

Many believers constantly struggle with finances. Often, we get caught in the societal challenges of materialism and consumerism, and we struggle to faithfully support the Lord's work. Regardless of social-economic class, people struggle with wanting and desiring more and more. This passage will help you reaffirm God's place above materialism and consumerism.

1. Interpret the meaning of "faithful" as it is used in the context of this text.

2. Does the text apply to us today, and if so, how?

3. How does this text support or oppose today's prevailing views on materialism and wealth?

4. How do we guard against placing the accumulation of wealth over the Lord's work?

5. What principles have we learned that we can apply to our lives?

Conclusion

We live in a time when many people are preoccupied with acquiring wealth and material goods. Sadly, some people are forced to take on additional employment or use credit cards to upgrade or maintain a particular lifestyle. Too often, when we work excessively in order to become rich or maintain a certain standard of living, our families suffer from neglect and the Lord's work gets overlooked. Our attraction to luxuries and upgrades often competes with our faithfulness to support the Lord's church. Jesus spoke often about money and possessions because he knew we would have many issues in this area.

Bible Study III

On the First Day

Background

The text originates from Paul's first letter to the church at Corinth. The church was located in a thriving commercial seaport. Paul spent an extensive amount of time ministering to this group of affluent believers. In closing his letter to the church at Corinth, he gave specific instructions on how to be in the spirit of unity with others who are less fortunate.

Text: 1 Corinthians 16:1-2

"Now concerning the collection for the saints: you should follow the directions I gave to the churches of Galatia. On the first day of every week, each of you is to put aside and save whatever extra you earn, so that collections need not be taken when I come."

God gives instructions on how, what, why, where, and when to give. In this text Paul gave clear directions on giving an extra offering to support ministry in Jerusalem. Paul subtly shared why the offering should be made on the first day of the week, and why special collections were necessary to the Lord's work in mission and outreach.

1. What does the Lord say to you, as it pertains to being a steward?

2. Why do you think Paul specified the day to give this offering?

3. What is the significance of that day, and its purpose?

4. Do you have any reservations about Paul's request?

5. What do you think was Paul's reason for saying, "so that collections need not be taken when I come"?

6. What have we learned that we can apply in our lives?

CONCLUSION

Paul gave clear instructions on presenting this offering on the Lords Day, the first day of the week. He encouraged the members to put God first, when to give, and to view giving as an act of worship. Further, he encouraged the church at Corinth to be like the churches in Galatia. Paul wanted these believers to plan their giving and do it regularly and proportionately, according to their earnings.

Bible Study IV

It's Only the Minimum

BACKGROUND

The text centers on the Pharisees, a rigid group of believers who believed the word of God should be adhered to as written by scribes. In keeping with the law of God, they believed in the law of tithing. A tithe is ten percent, so the Pharisees brought a tithe of mint, which was an acceptable herb believers could bring to the temple.

TEXT: MATTHEW 23:23

> *"Woe to you scribes and Pharisees, hypocrites! For you tithe mint, dill, and cumin, and have neglected the weightier matters of the law: justice and mercy and faith. It is these you ought to have practiced without neglecting the others."*

We live under grace and are no longer bound by the legalism of the Old Testament. However, we are still bound to give a tithe as the minimum gift to honor the Lord. Many attempt to rationalize their marginal gifts and sidestep their responsibility by hiding behind grace. In the early church (Acts 2:41-47), believers sold all of their possession, so everybody had plenty. That sounds like more than a tithe.

1. What was Jesus telling the Pharisees about their giving, and how would you have responded to Jesus' statement?

2. How do you feel about tithing as a response to the Lord?

3. Do you feel we tithe on the gross or net of our earnings? Why?

4. What would inspire more persons to become

tithers? And what is preventing them from doing so?

4. What have we learned that we can apply in our lives?

CONCLUSION

Many believers strive to become tithers once they discover the joy of giving. When people move beyond the point of debating the legalism of tithing, then they begin to find find joy in giving to the Lord's work. If you have not reached the level of tithing, make a goal of proportionate increases in your giving until you do. Remember, Jesus was disappointed in the Pharisees' attitude concerning giving, and in their failure to give adequate consideration of the matters of the heart and social consciousness.

SAMPLE STEWARDSHIP PLANNING CALENDAR

The purpose of a year round stewardship calendar is to provide a systematic approach to stewardship in the local church. Some activities take place weekly, monthly, quarterly and annually.

January:

Stewardship Emphasis Month.
Send thank you letters for previous years contributions.
Christian Finance Course.

February:

Begin Lenten season Bible study with stewardship focus.
Challenge members to make weekly sacrificial gifts during lent.

March:

Conduct an educational seminar (i.e., "Putting Your House in Order" or Wills and Bequests seminar).

April:

Send quarterly statement of celebration/contribution statements with letter.

Culminate weekly sacrificial Lenten season gifts or receive an Easter offering.

May:

Send "vacation letter" to encourage summer support.

June:

Participate in a mission project.

July:

Send quarterly statement of celebration/contribution statements with letter.

Start planning for Stewardship Emphasis Month (requires six months to plan).

Narrative spending plan/budget preparation.

August:

Educational seminar (i.e., Prayers, Presence Gifts and Service).

September:

Display a year-end giving brochure and promote it.
Educational seminar (i.e., Wills and Bequests).
Begin promoting memorials for All Saint's Day.

October:

Offer a Christian finance course.
Send quarterly statements of celebration/contribution statements with letter.

November:

Send eleven-month statement to encourage year-end gifts, and allow members to catch-up on obligations.
Thanksgiving Offering.

December:

Special Advent offering.

Weekly:

Offering meditation.
Bulletin insert.

Monthly:

Newsletter articles on stewardship.
Ministry moment.
Children's stewardship message.

Quarterly:

Statements of Celebration/Contribution Statements
with a letter.
Stewardship sermon.

Annually:

Stewardship emphasis month.

NARRATIVE SPENDING PLAN

Provide your congregation with it's own Narrative Spending Plan (see example below). Start with one or two representatives from each of the following committees, along with the pastor: Finance, Stewardship, and Council on Ministry.

1. Identify five to seven areas of ministry. (mission, education, youth, worship, music, and care ministries).

2. Locate a copy of your mission statement and the approved line-item budget.

3. Pass out and collect the narrative budget workheet.

4. Allocate line items into the five to seven ministry areas (i.e., allocate building maintenance, mortgage and utility expense, salaries), and put mission denominational assessments in missions).

5. Show examples of success and major future plans for each area of ministry area.

6. Write a descriptive paragraph for each area of ministry.

7. Prepare your narrative budget in a brochure format.

8. Tell your true story of missions and ministry to your congregation.

(Ed Engleking, Texas Methodist Foundation)

Welcome to Stewardship of Generous Church Worldwide

Thank you for your part in *Working and Serving in Ministry*, the stewardship ministry. God calls us to be the church through our prayers, presence, gifts and service. As members of the Body of Christ use these essential gifts to sustain and create new ministries, it makes a difference in God's kingdom. Together, your gifts and generosity allow for ministry to take place in your church.

"Where your treasure is, so will your heart be also" (Matthew 6:21).

Your financial contributions allow us to do ministry in the following areas:

EVANGELISM INVESTMENT

We are called to go and make disciples. This year we have planned several events and activities where we will intentionally go into the community to touch and transform the lives of neighbors. Neighborhood canvassing, concerts, spiritual tracts, and revivals are scheduled throughout the year.

$25,000

MISSION OUTREACH AND CONNECTIONAL MINISTRY INVESTMENT

Many lives were touched and transformed through our after-school program, food pantry, and the Senior's Spot ministry. Daily, fifty-five to seventy-five children receive tutoring and a nutritional meal. Monthly, over 250 families receive groceries from the pantry. Senior's Spot has experienced a fifty percent increase in daily participation. This also includes our connectional mission support. We foresee increased ministry opportunities to serve in the coming year. We strive to make a difference in the lives of others.

$73,000

CHRISTIAN EDUCATION INVESTMENT

In the area of Christian education, there will be an increase in Bible study classes for all age groups. Three new adult, two youth, and four children's classes will be added in Church school. Building Disciples has witnessed a forty percent increase in participation. Christian education continues to be a pillar for ministry in our congregation.

$16,000

MAINTENANCE AND FACILITY INVESTMENT

Our facilities host a number of ministries and events each week throughout the year. The practice of good stewardship requires that we optimally maintain our facilities. With the replacement of the heating and air conditioning system, we will enjoy more energy efficiency, which will reduce costs.

$32,000

WORSHIP INVESTMENT

Praise and Worship is one way to honor the Lord. It is also a means of ushering peeple into a closer relationship with the God. Our choirs continue to minister to the congregation through the music of Expressions of Joy, Gospel Singers, Youthful Praise, and the Voices of Tomorrow. The communion stewardess, acolytes, greeters, and ushers provide committed service for our worship.

$70,000

MINISTRY AND ADMINISTRATIVE INVESTMENT

Ministries are rapidly growing along with the increased growth in membership. The church has been understaffed for the past few years, so additional personnel will be hired to accommodate ministry increases and services. Cost is only a by-product of doing the will of God.

$140,000

Total $356,000

Generous Church Worldwide has a year filled with opportunities to make a difference in the lives of many people. If we continue to be faithful in our spiritual walk, God will bless us and provide all of the resources needed to accomplish this work. "For where your treasure in, so will your heart be also" (Matthew 6:21).

NARRATIVE BUDGET WORKSHEET

**St. Elsewhere United Methodist Church
200X Budget and Narrative Ministry Plan**

Ministry_____ Page_____ of _____

Contact Person _____

Phone _____ Email _____

1. Describe you ministry area. How does your ministry affect or change people's lives? How does this
   ministry relate to St. Elsewhere's mission statement? Tell a story and attach photos to illustrate
   your ministry area.

2. Describe your activities for next year and how they relate to St. Elsewhere's mission statement. Include an explanation of how funds will be used and how revenue (if any) will be generated. Attach an additional sheet if necessary.

3. Give an estimate of the total revenue/cost for each ministry event or expense item.

Event	Revenue	Expense
1		
2		
3		
4		
5		
6		
	Total $	Total $

4. Give an estimate of monthly revenue/expenditures for your ministry area during the ministry period.

	Revenue	Expense
January	$	$
February		
March		
April		
May		
June		
July		
August		
September		
October		
November		
December		
Total	$	$

(Worsheet developed by Dick Young, Texas Methodist Foundation. Used by permission.)

SUGGESTED READING LIST

Durall, Michael, *Creating Congregations of Generous People*, Alban Institute, Bethesda, MD, 1998.

Durall, Michael, *Beyond the Collection Plate*, Abingdon Press, Nashville, TN, 2003

Carder, Bishop Kenneth L., *Giving from a Wesleyan Perspective,"* United Methodist Communication, Nashville, TN, 1989.

Carter, Williams G., *Speaking of Stewardship: Model Sermons on Money and Possessions*, Geneva Press, Louisville, KY, 1998.

Crisci, Elizabeth Whitney, *Financial Letters to Help Churches*, Randall House, Nashville, TN, 1997.

Grimm, Eugene, *Generous People*, Abingdon Press, Nashville, TN, 1992.

Joiner, Donald W., *Creating a Climate fro Giving*, Discipleship Resources, Nashville, TN, 2001.

Jones, Clifford A., Sr., *From Proclamation to Practice: A Unique African-American Approach to Stewardship*, Judson Press, Valley Forge, PA, 1993.

Mather, Herb, *That's What My Mother Taught: and Other Ways Generous Givers Develop*, Discipleship Resources, Nashville, TN, 2001.

Miles, Ray, *Offering Meditations*, Chalice Press, St. Louis, MO, 1997.

Mosser, David and Brian Bauknight, *First Fruits: 14 Sermons on Stewardship*, Abingdon Press, Nashville, TN, 2003.

Toler, Stan and Elmer Towns, *Developing a Giving Church*, Beacon Hill Press of Kansas City, Kansas City, MO, 1999.

Toler, Stan, *Stewardship Starters: An Instruction Book on Giving for Pastors and Lay Leaders*, Beacon Hill Press of Kansas City, Kansas City, MO, 1996.

Vincent, Mark L., *Speaking About Money: Reducing the Tension*, Herald Press, Scottdale, PA, 2001.

Watley, William D., *Bring the Full Tithe: Sermon on the Grace of Giving*, Judson Press, Valley Forge, PA, 1995.

Weenink, Allan J., *Proven Resources for Stewardship Promotion*, CSS Publishing Company, Inc., Lima, OH, 2001.